legacy

ekua omosupe

. . . .

legacy

ekua omosupe

makua productions   **watsonville, california**

ISBN:1-887862-01-3

For information, please address:

Makua Productions
21 San Tomas Way
Watsonville, CA 95076
email: makua@cruzio.com

Cover design: Annie Browning
Book design: Annie Browning
Cover photo of the author by: Maria R. Davila a.k.a. Rhee Davila-Omosupe
Third Printing by: Community Printers, Santa Cruz, CA

Printed on recycled paper

I dedicate this work to my love, Maria R. Davila,
    in gratitude for her support and encouragement.
    She listened to me, we shared the vision of
    producing this collection of poems, and with
    others are able to present this book. Thank you.

I also thank my kinfolk, living and dead, for their
    visitations, visions, voices, and memories.
    Without them, I would not be here.

And a special thanks to my publisher and friend,
    Annie Browning whose vision and hands-on work
    created this book.

I have been writing poetry since I was twelve. At first, writing was only a way for me to try and organize the confusion and understand the alienation I felt in those lonely adolescent years. It provided an ear for my rage, my secrets, my questions, my religious anxieties, and deepest grief. But it was not safe. I hid my journals from prying siblings and my mother under the mattress, in my underwear drawer, and in the furthest corner of the closet. I hid my truth.

It was unsafe to expose myself, my emotions, to talk back; for I learned early that child contradiction of adult pronouncement was not permitted nor tolerated. Momma used to say, "Play with a puppy, he'll lick your mouth; play with a child, he'll sass you out." Talking back and questioning adults was met with harshness and threat. We children had to learn how to tip toe around language in order to be heard. Therefore, writing was my only outlet, though it, too, was risky. Today, writing and speaking out continue to be risky, especially since I no longer write strictly for personal consumption. I write to re-member, to record, to break my silences, to represent myself. In the telling of myself, I gain strength and support.

I join my voice, my body, my spiritual self, and my intellect with all of those who engage in this struggle to be free, to be visible and to be heard. We cannot live without each other.

Ekua R. Omosupe

Ekua Rashidah Omosupe

August 1997

C O N T E N T S

CONTENTS

legacy

ekua omosupe

My great-grandmother
    Mary
    was a willowy black woman,
    less than 5 feet,
    mother for 6 children,
    a lifetime of 70 years.

She was a sharecropper,
    grand-daughter of a slave,
    could pick 200 pounds of cotton a day,
    make dresses from flour sacks,
    slaughter her own hogs,
    she never married.

When Ma Mary died
    I wept for this fallen Amazon
    who fed me preserves and biscuits,
    rocked me at night,
    dried my tears,
    told me secrets about being a woman,
    how to survive in my blackness.

Momma. This photograph of you is so unlike you—now. The likeness is there but the youth, the shine to your young life is not as apparent, not in you now. This photograph has faded from black and white to sepia tones that remind me of sunsets at a distance, of drying leaves that have fallen from the pecan and oak trees that I remember from childhood.

Remember how we used to grab burlap sacks and cross the road to pick up pecans from the pecan grove. We would fill the sacks to bursting. You, me, Liz and all the other children. We would fill those sacks and make money off the white folks. We picked up the pecans and they would pay us 35¢ a sack. That was a lot then, when I was a kid, when you were so young, like in this photograph that I have in my head. We used to eat pecans like there was no running out of them; like they were in steady supply, as we sat on the porch across the road, after we handed our sacks over and stashed several sacks for ourselves for later. Those were the times I thought we would never run out. It was the time I believed in abundance, being full and not wanting.

Those nuts, Momma, their color reminds me of you. The hard brown shell, the stripes on the shell remind me of you. How you grew hard and cold over the years of struggling and fighting against death, poverty, too many children to feed, awful husbands and worry. You grew hard on the outside, like a pecan that lays too long on the ground, fades and grows rancid unless someone picks it up. People don't often look past the shell to discover what is inside. But inside, Momma, I know you are sweet and tender, and needing.

You were so young in this picture. Your pressed hair sweeps away from your face in a curly curve. You look directly into the camera, smiling, smiling, smiling, smiling like nothing will stop you. Smiling like you've seen the end of the rainbow; smiling like all the world belongs to you.

Your teeth are strong and white; your brown eyes sparkle. You are so hopeful. I love you Momma. You I love.

I look at the dress with its spaghetti straps and the way it fits your mood. You are so unfettered, so free, so happy in this picture, this photograph that I have in my memory. You look like a girl. You are the life of the party, your own party. I know you still have that young woman inside you smiling, filled with wonderment, excitement about living. There you sit staring at the camera unflinching, no worry, no holding back. The life of your party. The center of your play. The lines unrehearsed. You, Momma, were such a lovely girl. You were so beautiful, smooth, sandy colored eyes, hair, skin. Momma, this girl I continue looking for whenever I see your face these days. The recent photographs are a ghost of that girl. That girl hangs around the corners of your mouth, dodges the light in your eyes, but sometimes she almost emerges. She almost cracks your shell. She almost lives. I almost see the picture of her, her in you, Momma.

I was born in a two room shotgun house. My grand-mother and grandfather (the stepfather to my mother) were not elated and excited about the birth of this new baby. Where was my mother going to get the funds to provide for me? How did she even think that her parents were going to give her anything? Another mouth to feed. They already had seven children of their own. They had my Momma, but she wasn't John Christmas' child. She was born to my grandmother, Lovie Lee, who was no more than a girl herself. My grandmother is 14 years older than my mother. My great grand, Ma Mary, was only 13 years older than Lovie Lee.

What could they offer this new baby girl? Born black in the heart of Mississippi. Slaveocracy of the South. Born into illiteracy—poverty—sharecropping and many mouths to feed. What could they offer this new baby? This child of a child.

My mother applied to the state welfare department in 1951, my year of birth. The case worker gave her a lecture:

"Now, gal, you ain't much more'n a chile yurself. But Negras breed fast an' start early. Negras have lots of children. Now what do you expect from us? The state of Mississippi ain't bound to feed you and your bastard children. Y'all work and quit beggin' we'd all be better off. What—I say—*what* do you expect us to do for you? All you git is 15 dollars a month. That ought to be enough. I'll tell you, git on back to the fields. We ain't goin' ta feed you!"

"Get back to the fields—get back to the fields." These words rang in my mother's ears. These words squeaked from the floor boards when she rocked me to sleep at her breast.

"Get back to the fields . . . back . . . back . . . back . . . black —Get back."

She swore. My mother swore that the fields would not kill her. The fields would not finish breaking her back and her spirit. The fields would not break her in two the way they broke Ma Mary, Lovie Lee, John, Fannie, Jesse Brown, Lillian, Thomas, Buba, Uncle Jimmy, Bobby Lee, Miss JoAnna, Miss Carrie. The fields would not cover her in dust all of her days and cover her in dirt when she died. My Momma swore the fields would not kill her.

Mr. Floyd owned those fields that she and the whole family, generation after generation had planted, hoed, picked cotton. Picked it from the stalks; picked it from the ground where it fell from their hands—blistered, clawed, arthritic from holding tight to a wooden handle. They bent from sunrise to dusk and kept Mr. Floyd's pockets full to send his children to college. To keep his ice box stocked. Mr. Floyd would not bury her. He would not get much more from her. He would get nothing from this new baby that suckled at her breast.

15 dollars a month. 15 dollars subsistence. 15 dollars —a dollar for each of the years she had lived, sweated, been sick and tired—sick and tired. Tormented by the heat, white folks, cotton. What did she expect from them? What did they expect from her? Death was all they would give to this 15 year old because she had grown tired of "Yassah, Massa—No'am, Yassum." She was tired.

Her baby girl would not live as she had lived. She would find a way to leave. To take this child away from the certain misery that Yazoo County, Mississippi promised.

In Mississippi cotton was "King," a birth right, an inheritance for both black and white. The money that cotton put in white men's pockets was off the backs of Blacks who inherited stalks, dirt, tiredness, desperation, determination that often got them no further than town on Saturday and a longing for the North, a promise of something better.

I am the offspring of my mother's determination to leave Mississippi, cotton, mile-long rows, Mr. Floyd, lynching, Jim Crow and dirt poverty.

The echo of her heart's determination.

This child will not pick your cotton, swallow her tears, and apologize for being born Black, female and poor. This child will not clean your house, bear your bastards, wet nurse your children.

This child will not be your slave.

This child will...will...live.
    This child.

She is my baby
    11 years is not enough
    for her to know that growing
    into a woman Black and as
    full as the moon is not
    just a blessing

She doesn't know
    that there will be
    days, nights, years
    that she will dream of a girlhood
    gone too quickly

She doesn't know
    that this garden of
    roses and innocence will be
    choked by weeds and indecision
    monkey bars and swings could become
    cages and nooses and I will
    not always be able to fix
    her cuts and scrapes with band aids
    peroxide and kisses.

This child does not know
    that some of her hurts will become scars
    deeper than the black of her skin
    She is my baby girl
    growing too soon into
    a woman.

Community is the place where I was born,
 where I grew up.
 Momma, Lovie Lee, John,
 Isaac, Liz, Doll
 faces and names I can no longer recall.

It is Miss Betty,
 the neighborhood widow,
 raising six hungry children,
 stepping across the yard
 asking for a cup of sugar,
 a little cornmeal,
 or fatback to season some greens.

It is Momma,
 getting up early morning
 building a fire in the old wood stove
 to bake a pan of biscuits,
 cook a pot of grits
 and some fried Jack Mackerel.

Community
 is knowing the inside and outside
 of my peoples' poverty,
 thwarted desire
 and our hope.

It is the weather worn Baptist church
 at the end of a Mississippi
 country road,
 where cotton field meets gravel
 and every third Sunday of the month
 Reverend Miles,
 our traveling evangelist,
 preaches a tenuous gospel of
 Christ ... Salvation ... Freedom
 and we feast on
 fried chicken, butter beans, corn bread,
 beets, boiled eggs, fish, biscuits, lemon meringue pie,
 sweet potato tassies, potato salad, bread and butter pickles,

corn on the cob, peach cobbler, butter pound cake,
that my granny and everybody else's prepared
for that special day.

Community is
    sharecropping, caring for other women's children
    when they are sick, in child bed, or dying.
    How many children did my grandma
    and great grandma raise that weren't
    their own?

It is
    looking at who you are,
    who I am,
    sharing our stories,
    telling how far we have come,
    where we need to go,
    what we hope for.
    Can we get there together?

Community
    commune
    communication
    Come in
    Come on into
    unity
    make communion together
    together in our strength
    our weakness
    vision
    will
    So be it!

My mother's husbands are dead.
>She has moved from the grass hut
>into a house of stone
>where she grooms her daughters for
>womanhood.
>She tells us:
>hunt your own food
>slay your own dragons
>beware of wolves
>they surround you
>crouching in doorways
>blocking your paths
>they sniff you relentlessly
>break you like dried crackers
>lick your sweetness like honey
>from a spoon
>consume you.

Your steel wool hair
>will scratch their entrails.
>Your blackness will sicken their stomachs.
>In seven days
>they will vomit you up
>bitter bile,
>then
>you will live.

FAREWELL GRANNY
Harry Ruby Jackson-Hodge 1912-1995

I remember when I learned you had another name.
    I was surprised and sang it through the house,
    Harry Ruby, Harry Ruby,
    it sounded strange,
    a woman with her father's first name.

Harry Jackson had one son.
    You were his only girl-child.

Sweet teddy bear woman
    who fed us, brought caramel pops
    from town for "good" children,
    chastised us,
    advised us and loved us,
    I knew you only as Granny,
    a safe haven,
    an independent woman,
    who raised three sons and a daughter
    in the middle of a cotton field,
    without a man.

Your nurturance and affirmation of
    our self worth helped to bring us
    a long way from where we started in Mississippi:
    Satartia,
    Yazoo City,
    cotton fields, Jim Crow, back doors, and bowed heads.

You, too, thought life was promising "up North"
    Joliet,
    Chicago,
    Detroit.
    So we went.
    You followed and missed home.
    We teased you,
    The city can't take the country out of Granny.
    You paid us no mind and went back south
    every summer,
    a pilgrimage you would not live without.

Your round body,
    jellied laughter,
    unexpected sleeps, and periodic fussing
    will no longer be with us on this physical plane;
    you live in memory, photographs, and conversation.
    Your likeness is stamped on our faces,
    in our genes, indelibly.

I'm glad you had a long life.

You lived it without pretense
    and made something out of nothing.
    All of your children, grand, and great-grand
    believe in the miracle of you.

In 83 years you touched so many people,
    gave each of them something
    of yourself:
    a smile,
    a shoulder to lean on,
    some bread and gravy,
    a prayer,
    unselfishly,
    You loved us, love us.

We love you.
    So long, Granny,
    Sweet woman,
    Rest,
    We'll see you.

LOVIE ESTEEN MARIE ODUMS

a note to you at 7 months

Sweet baby,
    you are named of your
    great-grandmother,
    on your mother's side,
    a woman
    Mississippi born,
    blacker than a midnight sky,
    mother of 12 children,
    matriarch of your clan.
    Her daughter, Rose, is your
    grandmother.
    She began this generation of men and women
    from whom you have come,
    strong, resilient, survivor,
    at the threshold of this
    21st century.

You look through the eyes
    of Esteen Marie,
    your father's mother.
    He is an only son,
    you are her only daughter.
    She loves you.
    Her death in ashes
    wills you the strength
    of Phoenix.

Your birth into our lives
    weds three generations of women
    Lovie
    Rosie
    Esteen
    Their likeness is in your face
    when you smile,
    their voices speak
    when you cry,
    they dreamed you
    and gave you life.

My prayer for you,
sweet Lovie,
is ancient,
your baptism to
life:

"Be well. Prosper.
Seek the face of Wisdom.
Let her live in you,
So you may live."

I entered the womb
    of poetry

she made me
      daughter ... child ... sister ...
      to stars ... moon ... tree ... frog ...
      my senses keen to
      life ... love ... earth ... ocean ... hate ... death ...

now
      I know my immortality
      like prickly heat
      dry desert
      round earth
      deep ocean
      black skin
      dark night
      day

It is written in
      letters ... photographs ... children ... poems ... ancestors ...
      lovers of my life

This is a fresh womanhood
      borne of feelings
      intellect
      spirit
      genius

I move fluid
      through the days
      know
      I am writing myself
      woman
      poet
      lesbian

CROSSROADS
for Maria R. Davila

There are many of us
    who engage in this war
    of blood ... bones ... soul ...
    for the acknowledged right
    to live our lives
    the odds that gamble
    against our living
    sometimes overtake us
    and we settle

but

    more often
    we fight on the front lines
    of this war
    clothed only in our skins
    guided by the spirits of our ancestors
    warriors
    who fought before us

What courageous and defiant acts we perform
    the perils of death always confront us
    wait at each
    crossroad to liberation
    our strength carries the weight of thousands
    there are many of us
    dead and alive
    who act as map and compass
    sword and shield
    north stars
    pointing in the direction
    of freedom

We follow

I will miss your physical body,
     though I have never seen you in person.
     Just knowing that you were somewhere sharing
     the lull of
     humming bees on lazy
     summer afternoons,
     or watching sunsets and moon risings
     with me
     was comfort.

Your strong voice
     will no longer be raised
     in auditoriums to eager ears
     but your words
     continue to ring loud and pregnant
     in lecture halls, at dinner, among friends
     and enemies alike.

I miss you.

You always tottered on precipices
     thin as wire,
     threatening to slice you
     into pieces,
     wanting to cut your tongue,
     shut you up,
     but you stood fast
     and learned to balance your weight,
     carry some of mine.

You knew
     I needed your help.
     You told me to break my silences,
     confront my perpetrators,
     to look at my beautiful self
     and feel who I am.

You said, "I feel, therefore I can be free."
     I am open and trembling, Audre.

You told me *poetry is not a luxury*

　　that my poems are stories that must be told,

　　testimonies to the living,

　　songs for those who are already dead,

　　weapons on the front lines,

　　necessary as daily bread.

You taught me

　　not to be quiet,

　　to expel my rage

　　not to betray myself

　　for I would not survive,

　　was not meant to.

　　You taught me to trust myself,

　　Risk loving who I am.

　　This is frightening,

　　Yet, in my vulnerability I am strengthened to

　　face *eye-to-eye* myself and fear

　　that would make my tongue mute and my pen silent

　　in this struggle against dehumanization, erasure.

　　Even in your death,

　　You speak truth.

You did your work

　　Black woman, poet, teacher, mother, lesbian,

　　and invited me to do mine.

　　I will follow your example,

　　take the baton

　　and pass it on.

LUCILLE *(light)*

Lucille Clifton,
    light hangs
    from the corners of your mouth
    mixing with the darkness
    profound and revealing.
    Where you live
    trees and rocks talk,
    you prophesy.

    I learn from you
    Lucille
    Light
    that words are
    tongues,
    bones,
    blood,
    women,
    poems,
    spelled in brilliance.

    Spirit woman,
    Word witch!

Isabella
> was a smooth-skinned black girl child,
> born a slave
> on a Dutch estate,
> around 1797
> in the state of New York.

This Black Moses
> was born from the belly of
> a slave
> into the hell of white men's lust
> for power at any cost.

Isabella was property,
> she was forced to birth twelve children
> for her master's profit and watch them sold away,
> hear their screams for her comforting arms,
> protection, she could not give.
> She grieved the loss of her children,
> felt every wound that tore their flesh,
> their agonies mirrored hers,
> she felt her own mother's bottomless sorrow
> rising when she wept and called each of their names.

Slavery,
> white masters and their mistresses,
> meant to kill her.
> They tried to destroy this woman, body and genealogy.
> Somehow she survived,
> a charred Phoenix, marked by experience, the slaver's lash,
> and remembered in this poem.

I see her face reflected in this generation's features
> Our bloodlines are four centuries thick on this continent,
> North America.

I recognize her presence in silences and in my questions:

Have you wondered why we don't know her exact date of birth?

What are her children's names? Who bought them? Who did they become? How many of them died under the slaver's lash? How many of hers and her daughters' children call their master father? When Isabella refused her master's advances what was the punishment? What made her give in? Why was she deprived of sleep, food, and the alphabet? Did Isabella think of smothering her new born babe rather than suckling it? What prevented her from drowning each of them at first opportunity? How am I related to this black Truth whose voice is light now, a century later?

> The law promised her freedom
> > in 1827
> > but master
> > wouldn't let her go.
> > She walked
> > with a babe in arms,
> > before sunrise,
> > away from
> > a den of thieves,
> > threat thicker than night
> > stood between freedom and captivity.

> Deeper than her scars and pain from slavery
> > was her love of people and her desire for freedom,
> > her own and mine.

> She sought love and freedom
> > on her knees in a brush arbor.
> > Among tangled vines, insect bites, heat and fear,
> > she found God, refreshing like a cool, clear drink of water.
> > And she wondered if this was the same God
> > her mistress called upon at morning and evening prayers,
> > though she freely cursed and used her whip on tender
> > vulnerable flesh.

> Was this the same God who delivered Daniel from the lion's den?
> > Is this the One who gave Saul a new name?
> > Her prayers were a plea that she love

even her enemies, that her tongue
would bless, rather than curse, and truth
be her guide.

She was a black knight,
  Love sent to battle in the midst of white hatred,
  cross-burning klansmen, hunger and fear,
  with a bible in her hand,
  though she could not read,
  brilliance about her head, and a sword in her mouth.

Isabella,
  Soldier in the army of the Lord,
  freedom, love, prayer,
  her armor and weapons against
  hate/danger/death.
  She took a new name
  from the mouth of God.

Sojourner,
  black traveler
  through a strange land,
  spread truth like seeds
  in grounds fallow, hard, fecund.
  Her trek through the battlefields
  was deliberate and calculated.

Sojourner,
  Black Madonna,
  Saint for a diasporic traveler,
  Always give me light,
  Truth.

Pat Parker
    Poet
    Woman
    Warrior

You were born fighting

Your life
    a weapon
    which you thrust again and again
    against those who sought to destroy you
    because you were

    black   female   poor

You marched barefoot in the tracks
    of your ancestors and kinfolk
    who gave you the strength and the anointing
    to declare your right to be here
    In their names
    and in the names of those who would come after you
    you fought

Your life testifies
    to the victories that belong to us
    who are born in your likeness

    black   lesbian   warrior

It is a beacon for us who travel in the night
    hear the war cry
    and storm into battles
    that were not of our making but are now our charge

We must fight them for the sake of our survival

You fought a good fight on the front lines
    there is no coward in you

You stand
    a dyke at the crossroads
    of present and future
    shield and spear in hands
    encouraging us forward

a ripe
       pomegranate
       stained
       my brown hands red

       my blood
       stained
       white panties
       when I was
       10
       ripening
       into a womanhood
       seeded
       in a child's body

       10
       years old
       is not a woman
       yet
       I was no longer
       a child

As a child
    I began this journey
    to myself,
    looking for safe harbors,
    full moons,
    a bosom,
    on which to rest my head.

At twelve,
    I met Annie
    who was also searching
    for warmth, comfort, arms
    to hold her tight.
    We wrestled belly to belly
    on the living room sofa
    after Momma fell asleep.
    Our eager kisses
    and hungry fingers
    tasted warm secrets
    and sealed a pact between us,
    girl friends,
    who swore not to tell
    what we found between each other
    in the middle of that hot
    North Carolina summer.

We kissed and licked each other's
    disappointments and hurts
    to an innocent ecstasy

Until
    prying eyes and an uninvited guest
    discovered us naked,
    without excuse,
    in the middle of the afternoon
    on my mother's daybed.
    We were scared, angry, mute
    in the face of accusation and whispers

Funny . . . funny
You girls are not normal.
Normal.
Normal.

We ran from ourselves
　　and from each other,
　　enemies
　　who avoided each other's gazes,
　　forgot our pact of sisterhood
　　and girlfriends.
　　Rumors spread
　　and we used them like stones
　　against each other.
　　The distance between us grew into a gulf
　　and we each set sail
　　in different directions
　　looking for safe harbors,
　　full moons,
　　a bosom to rest our heads.

At twelve
　　we did not know
　　that there were others like us,
　　women,
　　who kissed, held hands, made love
　　to each other in secret,
　　our risk was theirs also.

I do not know where
　　this first lover of mine has gone.
　　I do not know what harbors she found.
　　I hope she is safe
　　in woman arms
　　and is lulled to sleep
　　with deep heart kisses.

I, too, have traveled far
　　and battle against my own fears
　　of being caught naked,

again,
by prying eyes
and shamed by some one else's fears.

On this journey to myself
at every chance
I anchor at harbors
that feel safe,
where women stand guard
on the shore
and lull me to rest.

I learn that safety is where we
make it
and I, too,
stand guard at the shores
of women's lives
protecting,
nurturing,
loving,
lulling them to rest.

the love
>you give to me
>is heady
>like brandy
>sniffed at twilight
>from a full round glass
>you weave a spell
>subtle as
>the kiss of morning
>on the mouth of night
>the more you give to me
>the less I am filled
>your love is good
>precious
>always tempting
>in all ways

I claim my
> lusty, strong, sensuous body.
> My curves and hips are landscapes
> where weary travelers have rested;
> my breasts have fed hungry babies;
> strong women have found shelter in my arms,
> some safety in troubled times.
> My Black woman self stands solid,
> a fortress against centuries of hate,
> yet is soft enough to absorb love
> when it spills from some smile, soft eye,
> kind words, embrace.

I have changed myself
> from fearful servant to autonomous woman,
> I am not the first.
> I hold my head high,
> read in the faces
> of other Black women
> who made this journey before me
> that I am brilliant and beautiful,
> worth loving,
> worth having,
> worth fighting for:

Harriet Tubman,
> Fannie Lou Hamer,
> Barbara Jordan,
> Anita Cornwell,
> Ann Allen Shockley,
> Ella Baker,
> some of them lesbian,
> all of them Black and woman
> determined to be, to grow
> beyond stereotypes and limitations
> to live
> companionship, friendship, camaraderie
> among sisters, friends, kin and
> lovers.

The Black woman who I am
    connects
    soul to passion,
    desire to intellect,
    spirit to rage,
    talent to pain,
    and births me
    full grown
    and coming
    into my own
    Black woman lesbian self,
    a wonder and miracle.

FIVE PORTRAITS OF MARIA

1

When evening comes
I will stand with you
and watch the moon;
its light
shining in your eyes
invites me.

2

Your magic
is your love,
serious,
consistent
like water on dry dirt.
I soak it up.
I pause at your
strength,
beauty,
and the sureness of your step.
With purpose
you hold me close
to your heart beat,
I listen to the rhythm,
touch it
without reservation
to my own heart
and feel day break
between us.

3

Night used to live
in your hair,
dark and impenetrable,
now
the moon shines
in it
and I cannot count the stars
that hide there
and twinkle their approval.

4

I have never known
anyone like you
seer,
friend.
Only yesterday
I heard god call you precious;
it was reflected in the smile
you gave to me.

5

I traveled
far
before I came
to your lodgings,
you invited me to rest
and you cradled me
like a child.

Lover,
    Your kisses and tenderness
    open the flood gates of passion in me.
    The tingling in my belly catches my breath
    and I swoon on this bed of love.

Between our legs is the sea,
    thirsty and salty;
    Neither of us is a stranger to her.
    She is to us
    what moon is to ocean,
    sun is to earth,
    sky is to stars.

Together,
    We swim
    her many rivers,
    our waters mingle.
    We sound the depths between us,
    touch,
    feel,
    the wave swell,
    straddle it,
    rush towards our ocean mother
    to lose ourselves in her bosom;
    Ride her
    churn,
    gurgle,
    force,
    to warm sands
    and singing gulls.

your plummed nipples
    strain against
    the silkiness of your shirt
    invite me to touch
    their round softness,
    caress their fullness,
    roll their erectness
    between my fingers;
    each measured stroke
    sends electrified currents
    to the eye of my cunt—
    a berry
    bursting
    in my jeans

I am Black
> dyke
> butch
> femme
> mother
> sister
> cousin
> child
> girl friend
> confidant
> lover

born from a
> girl
> who taught me
> how to be
> woman
> butch
> femme
> dyke
> bitch
> poet
> sister
> friend
> Bulldagger

IN MAGAZINES
(I found specimens of the Beautiful)

Once

I looked for myself
    between covers of
    Seventeen
    Vogue
    Cosmopolitan
    among blue eyes, blonde hair, white skin, thin bodies,
    this is beauty.
    I hated this shroud of
    Blackness
    that makes me invisible,
    a negative print,
    some other one's
    nightmare.

In a storefront window
    against a white back drop
    I saw a queenly head of nappy hair
    and met this chiseled face,
    wide wondering eyes,
    honey colored, bronzed skin,
    a mouth with thick lips
    bowed and painted red
    smiled purple gums and shining pearls.
    I turned to leave,
    but this body of
    curvaceous hips,
    strong thighs,
    broad ass,
    long legs,
    called me back to look again at likenesses of
    African Queens, Dahomey Warriors, statuesque Goddesses.
    I stand outside those covers meet
    Face to Face
    Myself.
    I am the beautiful.

Purple Black Brown Pink
    Thin
    Full
    Open
    Closed
    Wet
    Dry

Lips intrigue me
    make me think of hearts
    bows
    secrets
    pussies
    kisses

My lips
    are full, strong, supple,
    often painted Argentine Red

Once I thought them
    too big
    an overburden
    to beauty
    I sucked them in
    for the thin effect
    to join a standard
    set before me

Though tucked
    they would not stay
    intruding in conversation
    pouting
    stretching into smile
    insisting
    choosing to be

Now I announce them boldly

Lips
    my lips intrigue me.

Your surname
    has generations in front of it.
    You know your great-grandmother's
    father's father
    and how many siblings he had,
    the oldest of five,
    his face is stamped in yours.

Shikuma
    from Hawaii to Watsonville
    that name is written;
    what a legacy,
    a living name.

I was born in Mississippi,
    Black,
    a sharecropper's step-granddaughter,
    a teenage girl's first
    in a line of nine.
    Who are my great-grandmother's people?

I know my great-grandmother, Mary,
    her daughter, Lovie Lee,
    and Rose, my mother.
    There are no great-grandfathers to speak of.
    Where have they gone?
    Where are their names written?

I look for my kin
    at flea markets, yard sales, and second hand stores,
    there is no name to guide me.
    Like a collector,
    I buy the photographs of strangers,

Black
    African
        Stately

captured in sepia tones
    to hang on my walls,
    signal my beginnings.

Look at me.
    Do you see Africa
    imbrued in my flesh,
    mapped in the ridges
    and contours of my body?

Persistent strength
    and courage
    course through my veins.
    I am
    a testament to her power,
    life force,
    despite the efforts of white colonizers
    who try to cut her tongue,
    steal her strength,
    destroy her root and branch,
    starve her children,
    kill us all with
    pestilence,
    disease,
    prison.

I am
    blood
    body
    bone
    of ancestors
    who traveled in over crowded ships,
    chained to death,
    suffocating in feces,
    raped
    seasick.

Look at me.

See the resemblance I bear
    to kings, queens, poets, astronomers,
    mathematicians, mothers, children,
    who lay in the bellies of cargo ships.
    Listen closely.

The echoes of brutish voices
tell me that I am nothing
more than object,
instrument,
mule,
a beast of burden.
But beasts cannot talk, plan insurrections,
nor birth generations of Black African children
who look like me.

I am Africa,
  a piece of the continent
  displaced,
  a foreigner
  to my own people.
  African in America,
  a black landscape
  a colonized person.

Africa,
  a survivor,
  living in me.

COLOR BLIND

after reading Pat Parker's poem "To White People Who Want to Be My Friend"

There are people who declare
    they are color blind.
    They don't see *color*.
    They don't *see* color.

They see me.
    A Black woman
    dred-locked, thick-lipped
    a ring in my nose
    but no color,
    They don't see color.

Of course,
    they see that my eyes are brown
    my hair is black and white
    my skin is burnt chestnut
    rubbed red and looks like the sun has set in it
    But
    they don't see color.

Why do you,
    Color Blind,
    want to deny me my identity?
    Is it the kink of my hair?
    Do you think that if you notice
    it is uncombed,
    not straight,
    that I will be embarrassed?

Is it the thickness of my red lips
    that catches you off guard
    makes you stutter
    because they are so like the ones
    you have seen in
    Africa Adorned?

Why are you color blind?

Do you think I will be embarrassed
    if you notice that
    I am
    not white,
    not permed,
    not a replica of
    Aunt Jemima,
    Donna Reed,
    not like you?
    or

is it your embarrassment you fear?

When you see me
    look at my face,
    Notice
    I am Black,
    descended from noble people
    proud of our fortitude,
    resistance,
    strength,
    struggle.

I am Black.
    Black.
    I will stay Black.

If I have seven A.A.s,
    Three B.A.s,
    Two Ph.D.s,
    Live in a two story house in the good part of town,
    Own three Cadillacs,
    Ten thousand shares in AT&T,
    Teach courses in
    Economics, American History, and Politics
    At the university,
    Sit on Boards of City Council,
    Attend PTA,
    Raise "good" children,
    Attend church on Sunday,

when I walk down the street
    I am still greeted with

    Nigger

    Black bitch

America, America
> *God shed His Grace on thee*
> *and crown thy good with brotherhood*
> *from sea to shining sea.*

America
> Land of the free
> Home of the brave
> Equal Opportunity
> Pull yourself up by your boot straps
> Hard work is honest
> honorable

I pledge allegiance
> *to the flag*
> *of the United States of America*
> *and to the Republic for which it stands*
> *one nation*
> *under God,*
> *indivisible,*
> *with liberty*
> *and justice*
> *for all*

fairy tales
> the good guy wins
> always
> all ways
> the hero

custer
> nixon
> prince charming
> ollie north
> john wayne
> george bush
> bill clinton

America, America
    American Dream
    illusion
    myths
    hope
    wanting something better

dream dream dream
    what is this dream
    America
    Sally ... Jane ... Dick ...
    a white picket fence
    Mama homemaker
    nurturer of children
    Daddy home builder
    provides three squares a day
    works in an office
    wears a three piece suit

Dream
    Dream America
    American Dream

cotton fields
    three dollars a day
    pick strawberries, artichokes
    16¢ a basket
    "richest damn country in the world—
    anybody can make it"

Dream home
    Dream car
    Dream job
    healthy children
    happy wife
    money in the bank
    insurance coverage
    no more cancer from pesticides, poison food,

dream

no more internment

America

what is this dream

laws

lynching

prison

Stay in your place

on a reservation

in the fields

dead from overdose

in jail

You're taking our jobs

reverse discrimination

WHITE ONLY

DOGS AND CHINESE NOT ALLOWED

open a cleaners ...

Chinese restaurant ...

models of minority

Happy Dream America

no habla ingles

alien

disregarded

throw away

You have an accent

Are you stupid

You live in America, speak English

Love it or leave it

Go Home!   Go Home!   Go Home!

America

land where my fathers died

smallpox

Christian school

shaved head

no Indian prayer

rape
rape
liquor
liquor
reservation
starvation

America, America
land of civil wars
isolation
exploitation
death
hypertension
overextension

Dream
Dream
Plenty America

America, America
God shed His Grace on thee
and crown thy good
with brotherhood
from sea to shining sea.

*Chicano Park is a park in San Diego, California which was dedicated to
the Mexican People by the city of San Diego in 1975, after the city destroyed
the people's neighborhood to build a highway patrol office. The people of the
community managed to keep the highway patrol office out, but they were not
successful in keeping the property for their neighborhood. The city gave them
permission to paint murals on the balustrades that hold up the bridge. It was
their compensation, the end of an era, the end of a community that had been
there for over 100 years.*

Is this all the people get from
    the city of San Diego?
    A park
    with painted murals to
    replace their neighborhood,
    bull-dozed by city trucks—
    market racketeers—
    who needed a place to dump their waste,
    discarded automobiles, plastic containers,
    old tires, lead pipes, oil drums,
    toxic mishaps.

The people,
    la gente,
    dislodged, dislocated,
    nameless.

A park?
    Is this a monument to
    the people's history, labor,
    the neighborhood they built
    before there was a
    U.S. border patrol,
    to keep "aliens" out?

Aliens? People,
>who live,
>breathe,
>eat,
>work,
>raise children,
>crops,
>community health centers,
>resist police brutality,
>survive,
>struggle,
>and die,
>invisible
>in the midst of white noise
>and poverty.

For whom does the monument,
>Chicano Park, stand?

What gods of commerce and abundance are worshiped there?
>Chicano Park
>in the place of Chicano Community.

Chicano Park
>instead of a home in Aztlan for *la gente.*

Chicano Park
>a San Diego victory,
>another border.

AIDS

Frustration
  pain
  fear
  surrounds our lives.
  We are in jeopardy,
  players in a Russian roulette—challenged.

A thief enters our houses
  by day,
  by night,
  without detection.
  Infiltrates
  our neighborhoods,
  families,
  schools,
  churches,
  hospitals,
  our bodies,
  and sits silently waiting
  next to doctor, patient, crying parents, loved ones.

I am afraid.

The intruder
  sits down to dinner,
  sleeps in our beds,
  stands between our kisses,
  hears our most intimate conversations.

We,
  unsuspecting,
  do not know the toll it will take.
  Our very lives
  threatened,
  sacrificed,
  violated,
  wasted.

Who will answer for this?

the storm lasted
43 days
this rain
of bombs
is not natural
there is no
rainbow sign
no dove
to promise
peace

*Campaign is a term that was used by U.S. military and news commentators to describe U.S. involvement in the Gulf War. This term strategically camouflaged the real death and destruction of multitudes of victims.

CNN

My brother's face
    wasn't on the screen
    six o'clock news
    but he is one of
    "our brave young men fighting for our country"
    running
    from crack
    running from
    "death at an early age"

running
    to save his life
    dying to live
    on dry desert sands
    that sift
    his life away
    in minutes
    Kuwait
    your sand bleeds bodies

my brothers
    lay cold underneath
    hot sun

My stepfather is
    army
    green
    black
    poor
    his legacy of
    deferred dreams

drunkenness
    is written across
    a military landscape
    Germany
    Korea
    Vietnam
    Mississippi

My brother
>went to the war
>to fight for oil
>lower gas prices
>at American pumps

I sat in the living room
>watching the war on t.v.
>pin points of light
>scattered across a gray landscape
>did not show the black smoke billowing
>from your demolished homes;

the commentator
>did not talk about the poisoned water,
>bread rations, the fugitives you had become,
>hunted, frightened;
>they did not show
>the severed breasts
>fence poles
>shoved into pussies
>stomachs blown out by bullets
>leg-less children
>dragging stumps
>spilled guts
>and shit
>dead babies rotting
>in the sun
>stench/heat/death/maggots.

I heard
>Silence ...

silence ...

silence ......

Soweto
and Alabama are sisters
removed from each other
by an ocean
and a middle passage
both of their children
run in the streets
crying,
dying to be free

Afrikaners
white men
of Dutch/German/French descent
soldiers in government uniform
sanctioned and sanctified
in hate
convinced of their superiority
stalked black African children
in the streets
stood in the doorways
of schools
eavesdropped at classroom windows
shot them down in the school yard
because they wanted to chart their own destiny
honor their own heroes
be free

Those superior men
jailed over 8000
children
shocked their genitals with electrodes
raped little girls
confined them
solitary
laughed at their pain

In Alabama
police batons
crush black skulls
"illegal assembling"

illegal protest against
lynching/arson/castration/rape/segregation

"Separate but equal"
    stood in the school door
    wearing George Wallace's
    best governor demeanor for state business
    Spectators tore the children's clothes
    spit in their faces
    called them "Niggers" and "Jungle Bunnies"
    in the name of constitution
    religion
    tradition
    the American way
    race divided

blackness is threat
    poverty a death sentence
    democracy and freedom
    bad words
    punishable

yet cousins
    African
    American
    blend our voices

Muntu A We Thu
    Human Power

Amandla A We Thu
    Power is Ours

Amandla Ngwethy
    Strength is Ours

Men
        have interest
        in my body
        whether I hide behind
        a quilt of flesh
        or starve it to
        skeletal thinness

My uncle
        scraped my hymen away
        with dirty hands and
        a 15 year old appetite
        when I was
        a child
        not even six
        he made me bleed

fear
        made me nearly forget

my body remembers

In exchange
        for silences
        my stepfather
        did teach me
        the facts of life
        a penis
        that grew from touch
        to shudder
        and spit
        into 12 year old hands

I could not wash them clean

At age 14
        my curiosity peeped
        at white hands
        holding pink dicks
        that rode through my neighborhood
        to offer

five dollars
a ride
to ripe tits
and a natural ass

I ran

At 20
I married
My husband was a bondsman
held me loyal
with Mrs
a gold band
and holy book
full of curses

I defy them

God man penis
a holy trinity
secured
by feminine bondage
woman work
abuse on her person
forced silence
pain

I reject them

Mother
deliver me out of
this compound of thieves
seducers/rapists/fathers

Come tornado strong
in windy song
lightning in hand
thunder in your demands
Storm me to freedom
Save my life

once upon a time there was a woman
    who loved a man and bore him nine children.
    he led them into a desert of tenement houses,
    sleepless nights for children who had to stay awake
    so he wouldn't hit their mother when alcohol raged in his blood.
    he locked them up in cold rooms, there was no heat,
    they were hungry, sad, afraid of the father who hid jim beam bottles
    under the bed, in the ample pockets of his army jacket,
    in dresser drawers.

their mother could not sleep at night,

she could not get up in the mornings, she could not stop her tears.
    the man was angry with the woman, with the children.
    the man made them go away.
    they wandered through the streets, asking, then begging for bread,
    for a blanket,
    for caring.

someone gave the woman some seeds,
    showed her where to plant them, how to till the soil,
    how to make them grow.

the children worked,
    the woman worked,
    they smiled,
    the seeds sprouted.

At dawn she sits in the window, holding her tired body
    tense against her hunger for companion,
    her need for relief.
    She fears the quake that threatens
    at the pit of her stomach,
    an eruption that will unbalance her
    equilibrium, unleash the rage
    accumulated in pain, in suffering.
    She cannot take responsibility for the
    destruction that will follow
    if she slacks her hold on the reins.

Besides,
    she learned her lessons well:
    how to swallow rage
    until she chokes,
    how to disguise her pain,
    it might go away,
    ignore it, for survival.

Her mouth is bitter from
    demands unmade;
    they stick in her throat
    like fish bones,
    choking her breath;
    her tongue is swollen with fury.
    She holds her mouth shut,
    its wrath can slice men into pieces,
    destroy worlds,
    Curse.

Strong, black, and woman
    are synonyms,
    insult to her humanness.
    Her sanity,
    a tattered cloth
    wedged between
    anger and hope
    with her ragged memories,

a torn patchwork of men she has loved,
sold herself for:
3 pieces of silver,
a run down flat on 52nd street,
a dream
of love and happiness,
forever.

Where did she go wrong?
She washed their feet,
offered them paradise,
gave her body,
sacrament
on abortion tables in side street clinics.
The promises of lovers past
mock her
etching grief lines in her face.
She weeps.

The record of her love
is captured in
faded photographs,
yellowed letters,
musty sequined dresses in old garment bags.
Fragments of herself
rise like Lazarus
bring dried roses,
no salvation.

She nods on her stool
    a tin cup in her lap,
    a cardboard sign reads
    "I'm blind. Feed me."

Her head slumps,
    melts into the mound of
    overgrown, sagging breasts,
    that never suckled child
    nor gave pleasure.

A copper clatters in the cup.
    She looks up,
    offers
    a yellow grin.

My father was a staggering drunk.
    His thick tongue and whiskey breath frightened me.
    His words filled the room
    and his children sat like statues
    braced for each hard, cold, deadly blow.
    There was no room to breathe.
    How many times did we die in that small room
    of close walls and cracked linoleum floors?

My fear smelled as strong as skunk
    on a breezy summer night.
    In his hands it was a whip
    expertly wielded against my self esteem,
    a noose to hang me.
    I avoided his gaze,
    fear is sometimes stronger than determination,
    he drew me out.
    My daddy was stronger than me.

"You,"
    he slathered, pointing at me,
    an eight-year-old,
    innocent and timid,
    who sat in a semi-circle among three younger siblings
    watching, waiting
    for the fog of dad's drunken breath to clear,
    his mind to stop reeling,
    his red eyes to stop raking me,
    like hot daggers.

"You,"
    the word, as threatening
    as his hands around my mother's throat
    when he tried to choke her into quiet,
    stupidity, death.

"You—, you know what you goin' be when you grow up?"

I hoped he would say something nice, something good,
    like he said for Ronnie and Junior and the baby.

Ronnie was destined to be a prize fighter,
a man who would earn a title and make his daddy proud.

I waited for him to say something kind.

Junior was already a professor, a leader, or statesman
in my daddy's mind;
another DuBois, Hughes, or Randolph.
This was the smart one in my daddy's thoughts,
He is the one who carries my father's names.

I wanted to be something good in my daddy's eyes.

"Y—, Y—, You,"
my father stuttered again,
pointing at me as if I were a plague,
crime and cause of his distress.
"You know what you goin' be?!"

"No, Daddy. Please tell me."
I whispered.

"You goin' be a dumb street walker.
A woman who don't know her place.
A woman that gossips,
cheats
and ends up in the streets.
Dumb.
Stupid.
A bitch in heat.
A shame.
That's what you goin' be."

POEM TO RICA (MADAME TURNER)
whom I met at the BGLLF* in Long Beach ,1992

Miss Gold Lamé
    you stand out
    Diva Queen
    in full drag
    obvious
    as lights against the dark evening sky.

Your Diana Ross strut
    in three inch black heels
    swing your hips
    side to side,
    announce your intentions, persistence.

Head held high,
    shiny black hair cascades
    past your broad shoulders;
    you smile wide, warm
    invitations for some man,
    a knight
    in suit or armor,
    to love, protect, rescue
    you from invisibility,
    validate your womanness.

You say
    "I was Eric, before I changed my name.
    I was not happy as a man.
    Inside I am Rica."
    You show proof,
    a driver's license,
    social security card,
    and say you are thinking about surgery.
    "I live like a woman,"
    you say.

    I wonder what you mean.

*Black Gay and Lesbian Leadership Forum

She is flesh and bone,
   blood and marrow,
   a living being.
   Man is part of her inside and out.
   Woman is the source and nurturer of life,
   an incubator and teacher of culture.

Woman is made responsible for the woes of human existence.
   She labors against a bad reputation when she doesn't
   follow through with the duties, roles, expectations
   that have been imposed on her.
   Women punish women for not being subservient to men,
   for not being willing to lower their standards to male
   notions of who they are.

Who is woman?
   She is
   strong and weak,
   beautiful and ugly,
   determined and hopeless,
    a fighter and a casualty,
   mother-not mother,
   feminine-not feminine,
   good-not good,
   lesbian-not lesbian,
   whore and virgin,
   celibate and sexually active.

She is
   young, middle, between, and old,
   free, slave, rich, poor,
   handicapped and able bodied,
   hearing and deaf,
   intelligent and foolish,
   mute and vociferous,
   educated and illiterate,
   afraid and courageous,
   a murderer,
   and a giver of life.

She is

    fat, tall, skinny, short,

    happy and sad,

    a singer, a song,

    a seer,

    an insomniac and a sleeper.

She is African, Indian, Asian, European, Native American,

    Ashanti, Krew, French, German, Italian,

    Irish, Philippino, Puerto Rican, Russian, Guatemalan,

    Mexican, Navajo, Blackfoot, Cheyenne, Pacific Islander,

    Jewish, Catholic, Baptist, Spiritualist,

    atheist, Muslim, Pentecostal.

She is a fruit picker, truck driver, auto mechanic, educator,

    senate woman, judge, pastora and high priestess,

    congress woman, corporate leader,

    bag woman, homeless, displaced,

    grandmother, aunt, godmother, HIV positive,

    living with AIDS-full blown,

    dying,

    dead.

A woman is not too fragile to do a day's work,

    she works hard and endlessly,

    yet she and her children are the poorest

    on the planet.

A woman is

    beaten, knifed, raped, disemboweled, vivisected,

    fucked,

    and fucked over by sexism,

    belief in male superiority.

    She is not a punching bag,

    though often used that way.

    She is not a veiled wonder, here for

    objectification

    and ownership.

A woman is

    not second class,

not weaker than men,
"need somebody to hold on to"
hysterical.
She is not a delicate rose.
She bleeds, aches, perseveres.
Does battle.
Challenges silence, death, oppression.
A woman is more than you can imagine.

I am a woman!

I am black
> like the night
> that covers us
> and waits for dawn.

I am black,
> the underbelly
> of the earth,
> the iris of an eye,
> the canal
> that babies travel
> to reach
> the new world.

I am black,
> the world before
> creation,
> the beginning,
> the end.

> You must pass
> > through me
> > no matter the destination.

> > > Omega

is anthropology
religion
my momma's red dress
watermelon
pinto beans
corn bread
okra
fried chicken
cold grits
a stack of pancakes
new peas
a missed supper
little children
bare legs
bunioned toes
my short nappy hair
rusty nails
torn pages
discarded telegrams
a hug
some kisses
short skirts
tight jeans
Louisiana   Mississippi
Ohio   Connecticut
Black boys in Alabama
geography
stretch marks
a science test
22 people in a classroom
a pulled tooth
rain in my car
old clothes
my faded blue sweater
and
the list on this page

Q: What is poetry?

A: My sixth sense.

Q: How do you know?

A: I feel oceans move
      in my belly.
      Out of my mouth
      pour rivers
      waters living
      salty
      sweet
      sometimes bitter
      on my tongue
      as I sing
      black poems
      in the face of
      white out.

words
    swords
    spirits
    in my blood
    ancestor bones
    rattling my tongues
    to speech
    quickening memory
    longer than centuries
    clear as day
    sure as wind
    black as coal
    stronger than fire
    life
    creation

EVE, POET MOTHER

    in the beginning
        was Eve
        black daughter of Egypt
        scorned for words
        uttered from her brilliance
        courage led her
        to see if eating life
        meant death
        now past innocence
        she conjured words
        that defied an edict
        from god
        defined an act of
        resistance
        denied psychic
        captivity
        introduced her to
        the poet inside

    with fruited breath
        she spoke
        her first poem
        "I have eaten. I live."

In this land
   of strangers
   I call myself
   a name
   that is difficult
   for them to sing
   it struggles
   on the tips
   of their tongues
   they do not know its meanings

I sing my name
   of birth   Wednesdays   blessings
   my children know
   the chorus

dred woman

black

courageous

lesbian

mother

poet

warrior

friend

I am a song
   I do not hesitate
   to sing
   even among
   strangers and enemies

E • k u • a   *R a • s h i • d a h*   *O • m o • s u • p e*

E • k u • a   *R a • s h i • d a h*   *O • m o • s u • p e*

E • k u • a   *R a • s h i • d a h*   *O • m o • s u • p e*

Ekua Omosupe received her Ph.D. in American Literature from
the University of California at Santa Cruz. She teaches Writing,
Women's Studies and Critical Thinking at Cabrillo College in
Aptos, California. She is a former poetry editor of *Sinister Wisdom*
and a member of the NIA Collective, an African American Lesbian
organization.

Ekua's poems and essays are published in various journals and
anthologies. Her most recent contributions are to three new
anthologies: *From Wedded Wife to Lesbian Life*, eds. Deborah
Abbott and Ellen Farmer (Crossing Press: Freedom, CA, 1995);
*does your mama know? An Anthology of Black Lesbian Coming Out
Stories*, ed. Lisa C. Moore (Redbone Press: Decatur, GA, 1997);
and *Gay and Lesbian Biographies*, ed. Michael J. Tyrkus (St. James
Press: Detroit MI, 1996).

This is her first book of poetry.

The text of this book was digitally set in Plantin, a face designed by Claude Garamond and named for Christopher Plantin (circa 1520-1589), a successful printer and publisher of sixteenth century Europe. Plantin's strong, honest lines impart a simple, direct look of exceptional legibility.

The titles were set in Optima, a face both elegant and utilitarian, drawn by Hermann Zapf. Optima first appeared in 1958 at a printing trade fair in Düsseldorf and has been extremely popular ever since.

The running ornamental title was set in Linoscript from the Merganthaler type library. Linoscript is a registered trademark of the Allied-Linotype Corporation.